D1577813

The World According to Honey Bear

A Doggone Good Read

love,

Honey Bear
with Catherine Rodríguez, Ed.D.

Solo photos of Honey Bear by Tee Taylor
Oh My Dog Photography

Published for Parkinson's Association of San Diego in conjunction with Paws for Parkinson's ™

Copyright © 2011 by Catherine Rodríguez, Ed.D.
All rights reserved

ISBN: 978-81-909693-2-1

No part of this book may be reproduced, stored in a retrieval system, or transmitted by any means, electronic, mechanical, photocopying, recording, or otherwise, without written permission from the author and Publisher.

**Published by
PublishingGurus.com**

USA Office
5666 La Jolla Boulevard, #201
La Jolla, California 92037
USA

India Office
P.O. Box 12349
Central Avenue
Kolkata - 700073
India

First Edition

The World According to Honey Bear

Table of Contents

Dedication

This book is dedicated to all my moms and dads. First, to my Dog Mom, a Great Pyrenees: from her, I learned to be calm and to watch over the little ones. To my Dog Dad, a Shepherd-Labrador mix: from him, I learned to listen and to obey. These skills that I instinctively learned from my dog ancestors are part of what makes me a good service dog.

I dedicate this book to my People Mom and People Dad. From them I have learned what it is to be loved and cared for. I would do anything for my People Mom, whom I watch over as her service dog. I know that she would do anything for me, also.

I dedicate this book to children. The grandchildren of my People Mom and Dad always pet me, and Mom allows me to play ball with them. I am a pretty good catch. I collect tennis balls so I have plenty to catch. I even have pink balls with my initials on them. My People Mom is always buying me pink stuff. I think that's because people keep calling me a boy, and I am a girl.

I dedicate this book to the children at the Point Loma Branch Library, where I read every Tuesday. I do enjoy reading with the kids; they have helped me to write and rewrite this book. Thanks for reading with me! Besides playing catch with my pink tennis balls, reading at the library is one of my favorite things.

Finally, I dedicate this book to all folks with Parkinson's, and to the Paws for Parkinson's organization. I hope that this book will inspire people with Parkinson's to get a dog. We are the best medicine— better than anything the neurologists prescribe.

--Honey Bear

Dear Friends,

This book was written to describe the life of a service dog. Honey Bear is the service dog and the author of the book. It is written in the first person to give children a look into the world according to Honey Bear, the dog. There is humor and there is a serious side. This book explains Parkinson's disease and how a dog assists in improving the life of the Parkinson's patient. The book is meant to be shared, read with your child. Most of the book can be read by the child, but some concepts such as patient advocacy and neurodegenerative diseases will need to be explained.

All children will enjoy reading about the adventures of Honey Bear. However, children with someone in their life suffering from a neurodegenerative disease such as Parkinson's will be especially touched. This book is an excellent tool for beginning the discussion of "Grandma or Grandpa has such and such a disease." This is a difficult discussion to have with young children. Honey Bear and I hope that this book can be of assistance.

Catherine Rodríguez, Ed.D.

Parkinson's Patient
Honey Bear's owner, People Mom, and ghost writer

Who Is Honey Bear?

Hi! My name is Honey Bear. I am a Service Dog. My mom has Parkinson's disease. Parkinson's disease makes her brain not work quite right. Her brain tells her body to move, but the body does not move the way it should. It is as if her body does not listen to her brain. She moves slowly and gets tired easily. That is when I, Honey Bear, help her.

Sometimes her hands or legs shake. Sometimes it is hard for her to walk. I help her to walk better. I help her to walk in the city to the San Diego Padres games. I also help her walk across a mountain bridge that crosses a river in Yellowstone National Park. She takes a lot of medicine, but I help best.

I help her to visit schools. We like to read at schools. We also like to go to the library. We read with the children. It is so much fun! I love to read with the kids. I will continue to help my mom for a long time.

When she gets slower, shakes more, and has a harder time walking, I, Honey Bear, will be there.

"A dog teaches us a lesson in humanity."

~ *Napoleon Bonaparte, Emperor of the French (1804-1815),*
owner of dog Lauro, a Newfoundland

I, Honey Bear, am well trained. I started dog school when I was six months old. I went to dog school for two years. Six months old is half a year, and a good age to start dog school. In dog years, a six-month-old dog is the same as a six-year-old child. So it was just as if I started school at age six in human years, just like kindergarten and first grade.

The first two years of a dog's life are like 24 years to a person. That's like going from kindergarten through college in two years. I told you dogs are smart! After age three, we only age four years to each human year. I have completed four people years, which is 32 in dog years.

People year 1=   12 years in dog
People year 2=   12 years in dog
People year 3=   4 years in dog
People year 4=   4 years in dog
Total   =   32 years in dog

I had to go to dog school to become a super-smart Helper Dog.

This is my identification. It shows that I am trained and have passed all of the tests.

SERVICE DOG

Catherine Rodriguez
Owner Handler-
Assistance for Parkinson's
Dog's Name Honey Bear

See REVERSE side for ADA Information

"You think dogs will not be in heaven? I tell you they will be there long before any of us."

- Robert Louis Stevenson."

A Day with Honey Bear

My day begins at exactly 6:05 a.m., not 6:04 nor 6:06. The day begins with giving my friend and owner, my mom, a little kiss or two. I lick her face to wake her. I like to get up and go outside first thing each morning. The first couple of licks are for letting her know it is time to get up. But if she tries to stall, I lick her even more. Sleep is definitely over, Mom is up! She takes her Parkinson's meds, throws on some sweats and tennis shoes, gets the leash, and we are out the door by 6:15. We are off on a thirty-minute walk. I know that with Parkinson's the saying "Use it or lose it" is very important, and that daily exercise is important too. So I know that my morning walks are good for Mom; it's just that 6:05 a.m. is a bit early for her. It is also still kind of dark. Once in a while she'd like a break. One thing about me is that I am consistent. Daily means daily, no excuses! Luckily, it doesn't rain much in San Diego and it never snows.

When we return I like to stay outside, sitting in the sun to warm up. Then when I'm warm, I move to the shade and sit under the avocado tree. We don't have a fenced-in yard, but I know not to wander from our property. I only visit the grass front yards of the neighbors on each side of us. I also know not to bother people or dogs walking by the house. I just lie there, observing the world going by.

There are two daily exceptions to the rule: Jim, who lives down the street, and Debbie, the postal deliverer. Jim is a walker, who walks by our house several times a day. I require Jim to stop and pet me before he can go by. Like a toll road, he pays his toll of a couple of scratches and he can pass. Debbie is a little different. She drives the postal truck to the end of the block. I get up and sit at the top of the driveway. I watch Debbie go house to house on the opposite side of the street, then watch her come up our side of the street. As soon as Debbie gets to our neighbor's house, I trot over and wait to be petted and to give dog kisses. If Debbie has the day off, I just ignore the postal deliverer.

These are my daily visitors. Another visitor I like is Rick, the UPS deliverer. Now, I never get excited to see either the FedEx truck or the bottled-water deliverer; but when I hear the UPS truck, I go to the sidewalk and wait for Rick. He always has dog bones. I know dogs are smart, and can hear and smell in a world people can't even imagine. People don't know how I hear who is driving the postal truck, and how I know the difference between the sound of a UPS truck and a FedEx truck. But I do.

"Scratch a dog and you'll find a permanent job."

-Franklin P. Jones, American businessman

Why I Bark

Plumbing Problems

I almost never bark, especially in the middle of the night. One Saturday night at 3:00 in the morning, I barked. Why did I bark? My mom was sleeping. I knew she didn't want to get up, but I barked anyway. I should have been sleeping—but there was this noise in the bathroom that needed a person's attention. My mom got up to find out why I barked. My mom heard water. So she looked outside, to see if it was raining, I knew the moon and stars were out and it was not raining. However, Mom had to check, because my communication is limited. I can only bark, and people don't understand "Bark".

I sat in the hall by the bathroom door, trying to tell Mom, *Look here!* It is so hard to communicate without being able to talk. Mom asked herself again, "Why did Honey Bear bark?"

Then she asked herself, "Why is Honey Bear sitting in the hall staring at the bathroom door?" Mom was finally paying attention! She looked in the bathroom. There was water everywhere: a pipe had broken.

I had barked to let Mom know that if she kept sleeping, the whole house would flood, not just the bathroom. She needed to get up and turn off the water. Mom knows how to turn off the water, so she didn't need to wake up Dad. That was a good thing. He is grumpy when you wake him up at 3:00 in the morning.

Raccoon Patrol

One night I was sleeping, when I was awakened by a noise outside by the avocado tree. That's my favorite tree to rest under. There in our avocado tree were ten raccoons! I counted them *one, two, three,* all the way to *ten*. They were having a party, eating Mom and Dad's avocados. I know they like those avocados, because I got in trouble for eating one. It was on the ground and bruised, so I ate it. Unluckily, Dad saw me, and he yelled, "No! Bad dog!"

Anyway, I barked at the raccoons. They didn't care. But finally I woke Mom up. She saw the raccoons and went outside. Mom turned the water hose on full blast and squirted

those raccoons. They looked at her and said, in a raccoon way, "A little water doesn't hurt us." Then they went back to the avocado-eating party. Mom decided it was time to wake up Dad.

Mouse Patrol

I really don't like to wake Mom at 3:00 in the morning; she needs her sleep. People with Parkinson's have a hard time sleeping, so I try to stay quiet. This night, I was lying in the living room. I was on the sofa, but don't tell Dad. I was sleeping—but we dogs, we can sleep and watch what's happening at the same time. I was watching, and I saw a mouse in our living room. I knew Mom wouldn't like that.

I needed to catch that mouse. I tried to catch it very quietly. Unfortunately, it is hard to be quiet running on hardwood floors. I jumped up and ran across the living room floor, catching the mouse. I had him in my mouth, but I was running too fast and bumped into the wall. *Smash!* I was not as quiet as I had meant to be.

Mom got up. I was waiting for her by the door to her bedroom. Mom came out. Boy, was she surprised to see a tail hanging out of my mouth! She told me to go outside, and to sit and then to drop it. I opened my mouth and out fell the mouse. It landed on the driveway, a bit wet and scared, but not hurt. To tell the truth, I was glad Mom woke up. I didn't want to swallow that mouse, and I don't know what else I could have done.

I don't bark without reason. I am smart. I know when to tell people there is a problem. I bark to tell people I know something that they need to know. My bark says, "Come here right now." Hopefully, my mom will listen when I bark.

My Family

Mom

I don't know my Dog Mom. I know she was a Great Pyrenees. The Pyrenees are mountains in France. Great Pyrenees dogs are big and strong, and they help the

shepherds in the mountains. Some day I would like to go to France to see this wonderful place. Do you know where your mom is from? Maybe you could go there to visit.

Maybe your grandma and grandpa still live there.

I know my People Mom. She adopted me. I love my People Mom. I was lucky to be adopted by such a loving family.

Dad

My father is a German Shepherd and Labrador mix. Labs are the most popular dog in America. Shepherds are very smart and loyal. I am a good helper dog because of my Dog Dad.

My People Family

Mostly I know my People Dad. He adopted me; he is my father. I love him and my mom and my adopted brothers, sisters and nieces and nephews.

A man may smile and bid you hail
Yet wish you to the devil;
But when a good dog wags his tail,
You know he's on the level.

Cassandra, Eva, Honey Bear, Abraham,
Gabriella, Nathaniel.

My Name: Honey Bear Rodriguez

I think my Dog Mom's family named me Honey Bear because I am the color of honey. What do you think?

Maybe she named me Honey Bear because I am sweet, just like honey. Who knows? I guess my mom does.

Do you know where your name comes from? Ask your mom and dad. Maybe you are named after an aunt or an uncle, or maybe a color, or the name of a month or flower.

"The average dog is a nicer person than the average person."
- Andy Rooney, TV Commentator

My Country

Proud to Be an American

July Fourth is Independence Day. It is a great holiday for people. I like parts of the day. I am proud of my country and enjoy celebrating its birthday. I love the party. On our street, all the neighbors have one big party. We close the street off from cars and set up barbecues. We have games for kids to play. Everyone comes and has fun. The people eat lots of food. I smell the food, since I can smell forty times better than people do. Dad's barbecue ribs smell the best. I only get to eat dog food. Even on the Fourth of July, I don't get to have any of Dad's barbecue ribs or Mom's delicious blueberry pie.

But there is one part of July Fourth I HATE—and that is the fireworks! I can hear ten times better than you do. Just imagine listening to those fireworks ten times louder! You would be scared, too. I was definitely scared. My mom took me into the house and we watched television during the fireworks.

Remember never to light off firecrackers around dogs.

WE DO NOT LIKE FIRECRACKERS!

"Children and dogs are as necessary to the welfare of the country as Wall Street and the railroads."

Harry S. Truman

33rd President of The U.S.A.

Owner of dog, Fella

Presidents and Their Dogs

Presidents' Dogs

Barack Obama has a dog. Her name is Bo. Our first President, George Washington, had thirty-six dogs. They were all Foxhounds. One was named Sweetlips. President Lyndon Johnson had two Beagles. Their names were Him and Her. Now, that is weird! I wouldn't want to be called "Her". But I wouldn't want to be named "Sweetlips," either. President Teddy Roosevelt had a mischievous dog named Pete. When the French ambassador was visiting, the dog ripped his pants off. President John F. Kennedy's dog Charlie was the grandson of Laika. Laika was the first living being to go into space. I think that is neat, that a dog went into space before a person. Dogs are smart. I would like to go in a space shuttle. Or maybe I should be President. I can hear it now: *Meet President Honey Bear. She is the first dog to be President of the United States of America.* I would do a good job. I like all people and dogs, and I always try to do my best. I don't care what people look like, whether they are rich or poor, black or white, Republican or Democrat. People are either dog lovers (smart and good) or not dog lovers (dumb and not good).

President Honey Bear and

President Obama

Barack Obama is our President. Did you know? When Barack Obama was a boy, he lived in Indonesia. He had a baby crocodile for a pet. *I don't have a pet.* Barack Obama collects comic books. *I collect tennis balls.* I think tennis balls are more fun. You can do more with tennis balls. Barack Obama's favorite TV show is "Sports Center". *I like to watch "Dog Whisperer".* When Barack Obama was a boy, he wanted to be an architect. *I always wanted to be a Helper Dog.* Barack Obama likes chili and hates beets. *I only eat dog food.*

Every dog has its day

The Things I Love and Hate

The Quiet of Reading

On March 2, 1904, one of my favorite authors was born. His name is Dr. Seuss. We celebrate his birthday at school with "Read Across America". I love to read. I think that "Read Across America" is a wonderful way to celebrate the birthday of an author. Dr. Seuss wrote lots of books. <u>Green Eggs and Ham</u> is a pretty good book. I only get to eat dog food, so I couldn't tell you if green eggs and ham taste good. Have you ever tried them? He also wrote <u>How the Grinch Stole Christmas</u>. This Grinch character was mean. He made his dog, Max, help him to steal the kids' presents. They even took the stockings and the Christmas trees! His most famous book is <u>The Cat in the Hat</u>. Dr. Seuss has a good story but I think he has the characters wrong. A better title would be <u>The Dog and the Frog</u>. I can see it right now.

As you can see, I am a very busy dog.

But the one thing I find time to do every day is read. I love to read. Would you read with me?

These are some of my favorite books.

Work like a dog

The Noise of Microphones

I go everywhere with my mom. One day she went to a luncheon. There were some politicians speaking. I should have known better than to let Mom listen to these guys and gals! There was a delicious lunch, Mexican food. It smelled so good; of course, I didn't get to eat any. After lunch, these politicians from the city council began to discuss the city budget and the pension problem. This is a big deal in our town, and they disagreed a lot. The problem came when they had their microphones on at the same time. One person was supposed to speak, and then the other ones were supposed to get a turn. You know how to take turns. Every kid knows that. Politicians do NOT know how to take turns; they want to talk all the time. Well, when their microphones were on at the same time they made an awful noise! Remember, I hear ten times better than you do, so this awful noise was horrific to me. I sat there trying to be good. Mom even asked if they would be more considerate and take turns. They all said "Sure," and then went right on talking at the same time. So Mom and I got up in the middle of the discussion and walked out. Some might say that it was rude to walk out in the middle, but I say that it was necessary. My ears and head could not take the noise any longer.

A Dog and Pony Show

My First Plane Trip

My mom does advocacy work for the Parkinson's Association of San Diego. "Advocacy work" means she tries to teach people how important it is to find a cure for Parkinson's disease. Mainly, she talks with politicians and asks for money for research projects.

She also gives lots of speeches. One time, we were going to Sacramento, that's the capital of California. We went to speak to the State Senators. To get to Sacramento, we had to take a plane from San Diego, where we live. This was my first time in a plane, and I was excited. No one told me about x-ray machines and dogs. Mom and I got to the airport real early. She didn't have a suitcase, so we headed straight for the gates.

First stop: Security. We waited in a long line before we got to the x-ray machines. Mom took off her shoes, then put her laptop and purse on the conveyer belt. All that stuff has to be x-rayed. She was then going to take off my leash and collar, to put them on the conveyer belt to be x-rayed. They both contain lots of metal. The security man told her not to take them off. They didn't want me to be leash-free: they thought I would run away. They don't know how well trained I am! Anyway, Mom went through the machine and I waited. She told me to stay, so I did. Then the man told Mom to have me go through the machine, I don't know why. It was obvious that the buzzer was going to go off, since I still had my leash and collar on, the one with all that metal. But I did as I was told, and Mom listened to the man and did what he said. The Security men are the bosses at the airport.

I failed the machine, and the buzzer went off. So we went to the Secondary spot. There a lady patted me down, and checked in all the compartments in my vest. I don't think there is enough room there to hide a bomb. In this area there were two more dogs. They were handsome German shepherds, but they didn't have very good manners. They started barking at Mom and me. I just looked at them; can you imagine barking in a building? My mom had trained me not to be so rude.

We finally got through Security. Then we went over to the gate and waited some more. It was a good thing mom had told me to go potty before we went inside! This was a lot of waiting, and we hadn't even boarded the plane yet.

Finally Mom and I got to board the plane. We got to go first, so that I could sit in the front where there is more room. Mom told me to lie down when we were taking off, so I did. But while we were flying, I sat up and looked out the windows. There I could see clouds. We were flying higher than the mean crows that live near me!

We arrived in Sacramento. Luckily, we didn't have to go through Security to leave the airport. By now, I really needed to go outside, to use the grass. We stayed one night in Sacramento, at a big hotel. We were on the fourteenth floor. That meant we had to take an elevator to go outside. This was a lot of work every time I needed to go outside to use the grass. Mom and I visited the State Senate and talked with lots of politicians.

The next day, we headed home. That meant going to the airport, getting in lines, going through Security, all that stuff all over again. My mom's friend, another advocate, was coming home with us. We got to the airport, went through Security— everything was just the same. My mom's friend put her purse through Security, just like Mom did. She didn't have to go to Secondary and get patted down, like I did.

We boarded the plane with Mom's friend. While we were flying, I was busy looking out the window. Mom's friend looked in her purse to get some lipstick: but what did she find? She found two very large butcher knives in her purse! It seemed that she had gone to the butcher's to have some knives sharpened. She was in a hurry and put the knives in her purse, and forgot that they were there. So much for airplane Security: the people who patted me down in Secondary also looked at her purse in the x-ray machine, and didn't see two large butcher knives!

Where Has All the Grass Gone?

For New Year's Eve, we went to Big Bear (that's the name of the place, we didn't see any bears). Big Bear is up in the mountains. The first day was beautiful. We were in the mountains, there were plenty of places to run around and play. We were staying in a house, so I could go outside and use the grass anytime I wanted. I loved it. Then that night it snowed and snowed. It was very cold. I liked playing in the snow. But there was one really big problem.

When I go potty, I go outside and use the grass. I don't need a toilet, but I do need grass. The white stuff, snow, had covered all the grass. What was I supposed to do? Mom tried to get me to go. I went Number One and made yellow snow. I couldn't go Number Two without grass. I am a lady, and I can't just do this anywhere. I need grass, or at least dirt. We were staying there for four days, so this was a problem.

Every day, in the morning and in the afternoon, mom would get all bundled up and off we'd go to search for grass. We couldn't find any, so I quit eating. It is better to be safe than sorry! Finally, Day Three, no food, no going to the bathroom (or grass room), Dad cleared away a spot in the snow.

I was in heaven.

You can't teach an old dog new tricks.
"But I can get Dad to clear me a spot." -H.B.

Issues for a Helper Dog, a Serious Job

Going to the bathroom is only one of the issues a Helper Dog faces. Mom and I have a way of communicating when it is time for me to go out. I sit back on my haunches with my bottom on the carpet, and then I slide along the carpet as if I am wiping myself on the rug. It works well: communication without talking or barking.

My main job is to help Mom. We have good communication. For example, when she is walking, I walk by her side to set her gait. Without me, she shuffles and falls down. Another thing she does without me is "freeze". That's a weird Parkinson's thing, where her mind tells her body to walk, but her body doesn't listen and her feet just stop. I communicate with her mind by showing her how to walk; she just does what I do. If that doesn't work, I tap her foot to make her go again.

I also help my mom's balance as a counterweight. I provide support so she won't fall over. If for some reason she falls anyway, she uses me to help her get back up.

My mom is on the Board of Directors for the Parkinson's Association of San Diego. I have special Parkinson's Association jobs too. I am the spokesdog for the annual Walk. My picture is on all the Walk posters. I was on the television news. My mom was on the radio, but I can't communicate on the radio. People don't understand "Bark". I have a really big team that walks to earn money for Parkinson's research. I also got an award called the Spirit of Life. They had a real fancy gala in my honor. People got all dressed up; but I just wore my working vest and collar.

Why Dogs Are Important

Dogpatch

Do you know who Sadie Hawkins is? I did not know her either. But she lives in Dogpatch. Anyone who lives in a place named after a dog must be important. She has a day named after her, too. It is November 15. Sadie Hawkins was in the "Li'l Abner" comics. Poor Sadie, she was not very pretty. In fact, she was the "homeliest gal in the hill." "Homely" is a nice word for ugly. Maybe they name you that because you are so ugly you stay home all the time. Dogs don't worry about being ugly or pretty. Dogs are smart; we know that being kind and helping each other is more important.

Anyway, back to poor Sadie. Her father was a very important person in Dogpatch. He worried that Sadie would never find a husband. He was so important that he made November 15 "Sadie Hawkins' Day". On that day, there would be a running race. The unmarried girls chased the unmarried boys. If they caught them, the boys had to marry them. I think that is a silly idea. What do you think?

Dog Days of Summer

Did you know that mid-July through August are called "the Dog Days of Summer"? I know that these must be the most important days of the year. They are named after the most important animal, the dog.

Sirius is the Dog Star. It is the brightest star in the night sky. The Dog Days are when Sirius, the Dog Star, rises at sunrise. The Dog Star is so bright that the ancient Greeks believed that Sirius brought the hot weather of late summer. Do they have a People Star? No, but there is a Dog Star.

August 16th is the day we celebrate Saint Roch, the Patron Saint of Dogs. That is the most important day of the year. I think we should celebrate August 16th with dog picnics. Please serve dog food, no blueberry pies—and NO fireworks!

A dog is the only thing on this earth that loves you more than he loves himself. ~ Josh Billings, American humorist

The New Year

I am a busy and a fun dog. I like to do lots of cool stuff. I even like to go to People School. In September, I know school will start soon. Adults (you know, old people) believe that the New Year is January first. But for kids, the New Year is when school starts in September. When you go back to school, you are in a NEW classroom, in a NEW grade, have a NEW teacher, and have NEW classmates. That's a lot of NEW. I have a NEW backpack. It is blue. Some people think dogs are color-blind. That is not true. I know my colors, at least I know yellow and blue; I get red and green mixed up. I live in San Diego, so yellow and blue, Charger colors, are the most important colors.

On my first day of People School, I took the bus. I met my NEW friends. My NEW teacher asked what I did this summer. She asked that question because teachers always do. I said that the best thing I did this summer was go to the library.

The kids think the New Year should be in September, when school starts. The calendar says that the New Year begins on January 1st. I think that maybe the best solution is celebrating the New Year August 16th . That is the Day of the Dog, and it's just before school starts. What better way to celebrate? Dogs are the BEST friends to so many people!

The dog ate my homework.

"Not really!" —H.B.

Paws for Parkinson's ™ was founded by the Parkinson's Association of San Diego. The mission of Paws for Parkinson's ™ is to unite Parkinson's patients with suitable dogs, who will advance the physical and mental health of the people with Parkinson's through:

- Encouraging people with Parkinson's to exercise

  ✓ Daily dog walks

- Providing companionship to people with Parkinson's and caregivers

- Supporting the social interaction of people with Parkinson's

  ✓ Meeting other dog walkers

  ✓ Meeting other people with Parkinson's at dog training classes

- Providing daily routines for people with Parkinson's

  ✓ Dog walks

  ✓ Feeding dog

  ✓ Caring for dog

Reader Remarks

This book is an excellent tool to share the nature of the Parkinson's journey with children.
-- Dr. Ronald C. Hendrix, Executive Director, Parkinson's Association of San Diego

This is a great book. It reminds us of the importance of animals in our lives, to combat depression and to encourage daily exercise.

-- Dr. Ronald Kobayashi, Neurologist

Thank you, Catherine and Honey Bear, for a good book I can read with my grandchildren.
-- Tom Davidson, Parkinson's Patient

The book tells what the world is according to a loveable dog named Honey Bear. It shows you how the world goes, the Honey Bear way. It tells silly stories about dogs world-wide, and lots more. Honey Bear is sure to be the next Marley. The book even compares presidents' dogs with Honey Bear's favorite things! Children of all ages are sure to enjoy this carefully placed and silly masterpiece. Honey Bear and Catherine Rodríguez did a wonderfully marvelous job writing this book. I have already read this book countless times and it never gets old, from cover to cover. I guarantee this book to anyone from 0 to 99 years old! And so, in conclusion, the choice is yours to read <u>The World According to Honey Bear</u>, but I obviously recommend it! Go Honey Bear!

-- Abraham Cruz, Sixth-Grade Student

I think this book is a great tool in describing the dog's duties as a Parkinson's patient's friend, helper and partner in their everyday life. Making life much easier and more pleasant is so rewarding for both patient and dog.

--Frank Rodríguez, my People Dad

Honey Bear, over the years we have watched you have fun, be a companion, and ever so helpful to your mom. Now, we get to read your story. What a treat, and what a wonderful story you have told.

-- Grandma and Grandpa

Paws for Parkinson's and the Parkinson's Association of San Diego are grateful to Publishing Gurus for their generous donation of editing, design, formatting, and marketing time and expertise.

Publishing Gurus is a full-service independent publishing company with offices in Kolkata, India, and in La Jolla, California.

USA Office

5666 La Jolla Boulevard, #201

La Jolla, California 92037

USA

858-453-5456 (Betsy Gordon, Editor)

India Office

P.O. Box 12349

Central Avenue

Kolkata 700073

India

- Flawless professional editing of manuscripts
- Professional design and formatting of book interior
- Cover design by award-winning graphic artist
- Marketing and promotional assistance available
- Promotional book trailers available
- For an example, visit
  http://www.youtube.com/watch?v=biQVQCyARE4.

www.publishinggurus.com

The World According to Honey Bear

PARKINSON'S
Association of San Diego

Book Order

I would like to order "The World According to Honey Bear."
#____ copies at $12.95 plus $4.90 shipping and handling (for 10 books or less)
$____ Total

For quantities of more than 10 books please contact the Parkinson's Association of San Diego.

Books may also be ordered online at www.ParkinsonsAssociation.org and Amazon.com

Donations

I would like to make a donation in the amount of $_____

□ In honor of _____ to the Parkinson's Association of San Diego.

□ In memory of _____ to the Parkinson's Association of San Diego.

□ To the Parkinson's Association of San Diego

Donations may also be made at www.ParkinsonsAssociation.org.

Payment Method

Total amount due: _____

Check is enclosed (CK#) _____

Credit Card (circle one) *VISA   MC   AMEX*

Card Number_____

Exp. Date _____

Name on Card :_____

Signature_____ Date_____

Please send check for orders or donations to:

Parkinson's Association of San Diego
8555 Aero Drive. Suite 308
San Diego, CA 92123

8390833R0

Made in the USA
Charleston, SC
04 June 2011